CHASING THE MARBLEU

ALSO BY IAN MCDONALD

Fiction
The Hummingbird Tree (1969)

Poetry
Selected Poems (1983)
Mercy Ward (1988)
Essequibo (1992)
Jaffo the Calypsonian (1994)
Between Silence and Silence (2003)
Selected Poems (2008)
The Comfort of All Things (2012)
River Dancer (2016)
New and Collected Poems (2018)
Not Quite Without a Moon (2023)

Drama
Tramping Man (1969)

Non-Fiction
A Cloud of Witnesses (2012)
A Love of Poetry (2013)
An Abounding Joy, Essays on Sport (2019)
Inheritance, a Family Memoir (2020)

IAN MCDONALD

CHASING THE MARBLEU

NEW POEMS 2021-2023

PEEPAL TREE

First published in Great Britain in 2024
Peepal Tree Press Ltd
17 King's Avenue
Leeds LS6 1QS
UK

© Ian McDonald 2024

ISBN 13: 9781845235864

All rights reserved
No part of this publication may be
reproduced or transmitted in any form
without permission

For My Wife Mary Angela McDonald

CONTENTS

A Boyhood Walk	9
The Wonder of the World	10
Sketch	11
Colour of My Days	12
Tears	13
Paradise Plums	14
Old Moon	15
Whitecaps in the Wind	16
Brown Boots	17
Doing Okay	18
Notre Dame	19
The Red Flower	20
Dance of Light	21
Stealing Old Aikman's Sapodillas	22
Candles	23
Silence	24
The Lighthouse Keeper	25
A Death at Sea	26
Cane Cutter	27
Houston Blue Label	28
Green Limes	29
Chasing the Marbleau	30
A Good Smell	31
Young Gossamer	32
Eagle	33
The Golden Mast	34
Exactly What Happened in My Life	35
Bogass	36
Birdlip	37
Miracle	38
Half of Beauty	39
The Joyful Children	40
Rosalita	41
Even So	42

Climbing a Coconut Tree	43
Ebb and Flow of the Universe	44
Strange Morning on the River	45
Low Tide, Half Moon Bay	46
What Else?	47
Among the Hummingbirds	48
Taste of Water	49
The Day Starts Well	50
Rug of Fire	51
The Prince of Darkness Visits	52
Hardly Knowing What I Mean	53
Random Inventory of the World	54
A Taste of Time	55
My Wife Buys a Silk Dress	56
A Sense of Longing	57
Lilies of the Field	58
Sometimes I Hear the Rainfall Singing	59
Golden Oranges of Esperanza	60
The Red Locust	61
Of Course	62
No Tears Are Left	63
Alone	64
Morton	65
Strange Beauty	66
Hibiscus	67
Night Watchman	68
Falling Down the Stairs in My 90th Year	69
An Annihilated World	70
It All Begins Again	71

A BOYHOOD WALK

We made plans that sun-filled holiday
to hunt butterflies up at Mount St. Benedict –
not Marbleus – these are only found in dark river valleys –
but golden "biscuits" and treasures scarlet-winged and rare.
Tired, we got cool water and honey-sandwiches
at the Abbey. Sometimes the old Abbot greeted us
(we never dared say we hunted down God's creatures).
That day I left the others and wandered off alone,
down a shadowy path through old tall cedar trees.
I'd never been that way. Suddenly I emerged in sun
to see a green hillside dressed only in long grasses,
yellow pouis standing sentinel in the wind,
over-arching sky dark sapphire in the distance.
In early boyhood I had known unthinking joy,
now that lonely hillside in the sun,
imprints the knowledge that nothing lasts forever.

THE WONDER OF THE WORLD

No day is ordinary
if you describe it exactly.
At sunset today,
grasshoppers shone emerald
in the silver rain.

SKETCH

Alphonso Newsome, dougla with green eyes,
would offer roasted pistachios and a double shot
of El Dorado when I visited.
Tall, handsome, in his middle seventies,
sharp-cut white cap of hair, a noble figure of a man.
His talk was never commonplace:
how the moon looked ten centuries before,
of the Rowing Club on the Demerara River
where he raced the young men of his day.
One time I spent hours in his garden
choosing the most beautiful of flowers –
a white hibiscus with a crimson heart.
He would always hug me and say come again.
I saw him many times in imagination after his death.

COLOUR OF MY DAYS

Tuesday: emerald green – a vivid lizard glint.
Wednesday: biscuit-white spots of reddish gold –
humming-birds in a dull sky.
Thursday: a blue day, a calming blue –
pale blue of wrist veins.
Friday: pure white, not even a hint of ivory –
white as sheets, gulls slide along the wind.
Saturday: a strange and turgid purple –
the end of the universe, boiling and crumbling,
iridescent. Why? But it is so.
Sunday: blood-red, fiery orange – skies aflame
at dawn and dusk. A day to worship Gods.
But why are they so angry?
Monday: a sort of brown, a patchy, dirty colour –
as in a military uniform – some of Sunday's blood?
I woke this morning: no colour –
the world that shouts so joyfully is quiet.
A day to fear.

TEARS

It's no good sobbing for the dead. They're gone,
they'll never come back. A visit in your dreams
isn't the same as real life, of sweet love and laughter.
They won't return, they've left on an endless journey.
So let no tears fall from your heart. It's better,
so much better that grief be defeated.
Yet sometimes, when the moon rises and the last birds
wing for home, I suddenly remember those I loved
and sob for those who are gone.

PARADISE PLUMS

My father says, *Buy what sweets you want*,
and gives me paper money. I can't believe it.
Don't forget to ask for change, he says.
I reach up at the counter to put my money down.
What sweeties you want? the old man asks.
I point at the jar and boldly say I had to have my change.
The old man parcels up the twelve sweets I had chosen
and counts silver coins into my hand,
reaches down, smiling, tousles up my hair.
What gratitude, what eager, excited joy,
sweets of red and gold, dusted with white sugar!
Paradise plums I remember them being called.
Suck one now and all childhood comes alive.

OLD MOON

Dull, lopsided rock in the sky,
bruised, rotten-orange tint,
It drops slowly in the black sea,
all its gold and silver travels spent.

WHITE CAPS IN THE WIND

White caps in the river wind;
in the distance of the deep blue sky
golden-veiled cloud-caverns drift;
birds in their beauty fly as if dancing;
the children laugh on the golden beach;
sun-parrots fly from the green forest.
In simple happiness, my heart lifts and leaps;
I cannot count the blessings of this day.
When night comes, the sky's necklace,
pebbles of silver, shines in the dark river;
a great peace comes over the world.
Is it forever this, will it keep and last?
I breathe the sweet wind long and deep,
raise my hands in praise and prayer.

BROWN BOOTS

Outside the gardener's storage room,
a pair of brown boots soak in the rain.
Inside, Ram's kit – cutlasses, cow-milking stool.
Though often rum-soaked, my mother
held him dear; he was blessed with laughter,
played hide-and-seek with her little boy.
A pair of brown boots in the rain,
unused in all his barefoot years.

DOING OKAY

So much he dared and luckily surmounted,
a perilous life of marvels and scrapes,
a cavalcade of fun, descents into desperation.
I have loved him for his life packed to overflowing,
the kindness that kept him free from human spite.
When we meet again, age has got him:
bones frail, ice-shuffle in his walk,
my shoulder gripped for steadiness;
the fat women of his life have all begun to sing.
When I ask him how he is: *Doing okay*,
he says quietly, eyes still smiling bright,

NOTRE DAME

I have worshipped under old heavens,
prayed in great cathedrals,
bathed in the crimson sunlight
let in through tall, stained-glass casements,
heard their well-trained choirs sing –
such a sense of joy and wonder.
On the river now, the sun rises golden-red,
a young girl, smiling, bathes her baby,
softly sings, not seeing me.
Her lullaby breaks my ancient heart.

THE RED FLOWER

Travelling down to Parika on the Essequibo,
the dawn's gleam sweeping over the wide water,
I've always loved that perfect morning light,
shining cloud castles in the immense sky.
Close to the bank, the forest wall dark green,
trees tall as cathedrals where hawks and eagles fly,
I see a red flower blossoming high in the trees.
We stop, turn the boat around, nose into the bank.
The boatman, who knows everything, cannot name the flower.
Too high to climb, we have to leave it there.
In that dark green shadow, the flower flamed so strangely.
What is in me that cannot forget that blossoming,
a hundred times travelled there, never seen again?

DANCE OF LIGHT

A favourite place was Caura River:
water clear and pure ran there,
black rocks in the silver stream;
girls collecting lady slippers,
skins of ebony shining in the sun;
birds whistling in the green-tree caverns,
rare Marbleu! Ah my racing heart!

STEALING OLD AIKMAN'S SAPODILLAS

A faded forearm scar whose cause I can't forget –
a zig-zag pattern looking like an S –
I'd gone with boyhood boldness and my best of friends
to steal sweet sapodillas from the orchard next to us.
Suddenly, we saw old Aikman at his door,
and scrambled back over the barbed-wire fence,
daring robbers escaping from his grasp.
My arm ripped, spilled blood excitingly.
I wrapped it with a pocket handkerchief,
told lies to my mother, the blood vivid,
swirling in the alabaster basin.
Later, the old man, told us,
Take all you want, my sons.
Small wounds make long memories.

CANDLES

When I was young, teenage years, perhaps,
I and my friend Colin experimented with candles.
We put them in the open blaze of noonday sun,
when there was a full moon and when no moon;
placed candles to shine in bottles of all colours –
dramatic blood-red was our favourite one;
measured how long a single candle took to heat
a cup of water – all this written in a blue-covered
King George notebook. Recollection so exact
astounds me to this day. And there is a picture
of Colin with a lit candle standing solemnly
in front of a bonfire roaring red.
What on earth was all this for, I wonder.
These days, whats and whys come so readily to mind:
why I recall how long ago a neighbour's little girl
would cry all day as if her heart would break.

SILENCE

I walk alone among sea-birds
in this graveyard sloping to the sea —
a sheet of gold at sunset.
Small green leaves of mahogany trees
overhang moss-mottled gravestones
fearsome in their silence.
It is a long time since I spoke with those I loved.

THE LIGHTHOUSE KEEPER

On holiday, down at Toco beach,
we'd visit the lighthouse keeper in his tower,
cranky, old, but he had tales to tell.
We'd gather round, flies attracted
to a brimming honey pot:
miracles, amazements, mysteries of the sea.
We liked best his grim declarations
when dooms so vividly foreseen were alien to us.
After life is not death, he declared.
After life is nothing – slamming down his fist.
But then he had a silver needle handy
to show how hard heaven was to enter,
especially for us, the pampered of the world.
What about yourself, Mr. Lighthouse Keeper?
He liked that question to be put to him,
and swept his eyes across the vast and jewelled night.
I will travel far among the hottest stars of hell.

A DEATH AT SEA

They found him on the muddy foreshore,
clinging to a piece of driftwood,
he'd died not long before, afloat for days they said.
Mangrove crabs were crawling on him.
The morgue reports his lips were blue.
Pictures show him handsome, smiling,
a young man, no more than his late teens,
fingering a locket at his neck.
He wanted to try something,
earn money, see the world, adventure.
They say he fought hard for life;
his fingers had to be prised
from the soaked tree-branch.
He fought for life; I can't forget that report.
He was not my son, but tears were in my eyes.
I wish to God he'd won that fight.

CANE-CUTTER

Still living in the old, dilapidated ranges,
he well could talk of the trials of the years,
how he cut himself in the fields – limp-hopped
his life thereafter. How he was always in trouble
with authority, protesting the crop bonus not enough –
not paid for obstacles in the cane. He'd been
charged before the courts – just disreputable
behaviour. He'd wed a sweet li'l girl,
roti and shrimp curry she prepare good,
but she died, and he never had children
that he knew about. Was work, work, work.
Worst work was cleaning the side canal,
weed thick like the Sargasso Sea. Plenty water-snakes –
two friends done dead. Cutting cane not so bad
in early morning, but, oh God, the sun hot in truth!
Then it was good resting in tree shade,
watching sparrow hawk float in the sky,
laughing cricket talk with the boys,
new king Rohan, boss bat of the land.
Taking it easy, man, life could be sweet,
and he not saying he didn't take up his rum,
never pelt a chop or bus' anyone head.
Man, I even get name "separator", he say.
One time he summed it all up: *I born and I die
like any man does. I get what I get, I give
what I give, that is how I know I live.*
After eighteen years, they put him aside.
He ask himself what he must do
because he still had years to go before he die,
and so he became a carver of wood.
He made me a fine piece and I paid him well –
a man on a horse in dark purpleheart.
For years, I've kept him in sight on my desk.
For no reason, you'd think, I call him Cervantes.

HOUSTON BLUE LABEL

Balthasar, short, square, solid as a rock,
black eyebrows cut straight across.
As a young man they called him Stalin
when he grew a famous big moustache.
When he laugh, he laugh big.
I enjoyed our weekly conversations
in his green tall house veranda,
his hammock swinging while I sat
in the wind so sweet down old Brickdam,
first mud street paved centuries ago.
He told me that he knew the story
of our favoured rum, "Houston Blue",
with its smooth unforgettable kick and kiss,
by far the best rum in the land.
He had known the old man well,
and tried to get the unwritten secret mix.
My friend, he said, *the treasure died with him.*
All Old Houston tell me when he'd had a few
was nutmeg in the fermentation, then his mouth
shut like a trap. After Houston died and stocks
were low, my friend say he left sudden
from Houston's funeral Mass. He raised his glass
and shook with laughter: *I go buy all the cases*
I could get, but still, I have to limit you!

GREEN LIMES ON THE KITCHEN TABLE

A friend told me when I was very young
that should I cut or bruise in some mishap,
slice a green lime and rub it on the place:
sting like damn but it will mend you.
Green limes picked fresh from the garden
open up the gates of boyhood.

CHASING THE MARBLEU

Out of the green dark, the river runs
into light, gold-spangled by the sun,
and a vivid marbleu flies out of the thicket,
zig-zags along the racing river,
flashing sapphire. Caught, if that should ever happen,
it represented the wealth of all the Indies.
I chased him stumbling – what a prize to gain!
Yet when he escaped, flying fast across
the tumult of the river, it almost didn't matter.
I remember laughing at the pure joy of it,
young health knowing life would never end,
animal spirits at the peak of form.
Loss was not an option when living was so true.
One day you'll get him, friends kindly assured me.
There'll never be a next time just like that, I knew.

A GOOD SMELL

I still don't know what the scent
was that morning –
pleasant, soothing, not sharp, fragrant.
It wasn't any flower in the garden,
or rain on hot grass – no, I knew those well.
Could it possibly have been
a fugitive breeze from heaven,
made-up, sacramental,
or the man who passed selling watermelons,
or just the – sometimes – good smell of life?

YOUNG GOSSAMER

Unkempt, uncouth villain of a youth,
he came to our back door looking for work.
I nearly turned him out, said *Get yourself a wash,*
but must have seen some God-given thing in him.
Who knows, nothing's sure until it happens.
Young workless Ryan Cumberbatch Gossamer,
thirty years now I can't do without him,
all the jobs he's done, all the skills he's learned.
That boy, the first day he came, no father, mother,
tossed from home to home, he had a gift
beyond value – his desperate desire to learn,
if anyone would teach him. Now he tends
the fruit and herbs, knows the tailor, shoe repairer,
paints the walls of home. Early on he learned to drive –
now I go nowhere without him. My children's children
are his own; he guards them with his life.
Now I am old and stumbling, he supports me to and fro.
When I get sick, fear grows in his eyes.
I don't know what he'll do when I die. I've
told the children, look after him, young Gossamer,
uncouth youth of all those years ago.

EAGLE

A bad thing happened one morning,
a neat-suited young man at the gate
had a fierce-eyed eagle taller than its cage
for sale – one hundred US dollars.
What would I do with an eagle? I asked the man,
but when he was out-of-sight, this cramped
sky-climber caught my heart.
Of course, of course, one hundred dollars buys
him heaven's freedom, dives and soars exulting.

THE GOLDEN MAST

At 84, Dundonald Street,
Grandma told me a story once,
and only once, how
a young boy went to sea
pretending to be a man.
This brave adventurer
had found the way
to a ship's hull built of English oak,
deck of strong pitch-pine,
billowing sails of sturdy cloth.
So finely was it made, my child,
it even had a golden mast,
a vessel fit for kings and queens.
It was the good ship's maiden voyage
when three days out of harbour-safety
storms blew and the ship could not withstand it.
Waves roared higher than deck
of strong pitch-pine, soon broke
the hull of English oak.
The ship was sinking fast, my child.
The only hope the boy could see
was the tall mast he could cling to.
You know the story's end, my child.
Gold sinks the same as worthless stone.

EXACTLY WHAT HAPPENED IN MY LIFE

I touched the sleeve of the old Pope once,
saw gold thread woven in his white robe.
I met Her Gracious Majesty the Queen;
she talked about the palace plumbing.
Sitting down to lunch last Sunday
I brushed away two flies settled on my clean plate.
I took the plate to the kitchen sink,
washed it under a stream of hot water,
dried it with a hand towel, hibiscus-patterned,
went back to the table and helped myself to the pilau.
This I know absolutely happened in my life.

BOGASS

Old Bogass loved his cats but pelted stones at people.
He was not so old, but his hair was white.
He had a woman, his beloved, his everything.
When she died, he lived bitterly alone
in a bruk-up logie in the Rose Hall sugar ranges.
I got to know him as a keen young manager,
grew to know his case but doubt he cared for me at all.
I tried to help him, offered good housing
but he scorned handouts, chased me and others out.
He would live alone in that derelict hut he painted red,
planted flowers all around and golden apple trees.
He came to tolerate me when I paid unofficial visits,
and liked to tell stories as cats weaved between his legs.
When he grew deathly sick he would not go to any clinic,
but got a message to me find his cats a home.
When he died his body flamed on a scented pyre.
He left money for that and asked that his ashes
be scattered on his beloved's grave, now so lost
I had trouble finding it. The rest floated
far far out to sea where the big winds are.

BIRDLIP

Bracewell – "I like the name, it strong" –
lived at the edge of Industry allotment
a programme begun when he was young.
There he planted vegetables and cherry trees,
raised fowls and pigs, earned just enough.
His house, at first no more than a small shelter,
he slowly added living rooms and kitchen space,
and a bathroom far beyond nearby dishevelments.
There he raised a family with his neat and tidy wife,
with whom he lived in love and grace,
three boys who grew straight and steady.
One became a bank manager; all played
good club cricket. I met Bracewell at a Bourda Test,
and we got talking, exulting as we watched
West Indies win. We became friends
and I visited him often at the run-down
edge of Industry. He told me when he
was young they named him Birdlip for his songs.
Some high-ups told him he was good but he
never had the time or wish to pursue this.
I asked him once if he felt regret; he
shook his head, laughed that it was chupidness.
But there was one recording his sons
made long ago, and had kept safe. The sound
was clear, tentative and fading. What secrets do
such lives conceal? We never know for sure.

MIRACLE

The day was searing hot, the sky intense blue.
Anxious – we could see the blaze from our balcony
just below the Abbey, roaring red, expanding –
I asked my father/mother what caused the fire
on the mountainside, tinder-dry for months.
A careless fallen match – could have been
the Abbot smoking, my father said.
My mother frowned at him. I said it
looked as if St. Benedict's holy walls would go.
Would they survive another day's engulfing flames?
Son, you forget divine intervention.
My father smiled at my mother and me.
That night heavy rain fell across the Northern Range

HALF OF BEAUTY

My eyes fail me in old age,
I told my friend one day
I see about half of everything.
Be blessed, my brother, he said,
half of beauty is still a lot.

THE JOYFUL CHILDREN

Years ago – thirty, even forty –
walking in the park, cool at evening time,
I saw two children playing, a girl and boy, about ten,
laughing, pointing with delight at green parrots
flying low towards the sea wall. Look, look!
They caught each other, danced and laughed,
skipped and laughed, made me laugh myself.
Under green shade trees they raced and rested
until the gateman came to close the park.
What happened to those joyful children?
Again, before my eyes, they skip and dance.
Pray everything turned out well for them.

ROSALITA

An old, bowed East Indian woman,
Rosalita – I never knew another name –
was always at the Cathedral of the Sacred Heart.
With features that had once been beautiful,
she dressed in unvaried white and black,
except a red brooch always at her throat,
her grey hair tangled in a makeshift kerchief.
An age ago when she was young she'd loved
a champion cyclist who died exhausted
on a practice ride. She'd had with him
twin teenage sons, tall and handsome, whom
she adored. They died cruelly in successive years –
though I don't know what fate chose for them.
She had nothing, no one. How she didn't go mad
is beyond belief. I knew her twenty years or more.
The Jesuit fathers told her story – old Father Brown,
bent all askew in age, young Tony Metcalf, the pilot-priest.
They'd found her in her daily sorrow, gave her
God's work to do, arranging candles for the holy days.
You could always find her in the side chapel
of the Virgin Mary, on her knees – imploring what?
The bishop blessed her as a child of God –
a little ceremony I attended. She took
care of the Sunday candles, consulted where
flowers should be put. Three days a year the priests
allowed her red candles on the Virgin's altar.
It's not that I ever got to know her, saw
only what seemed life's desperate sadness,
and how memory must be made into a shrine forever,
or become a space where demons hide.
When she began to fade, forget, complain,
she became a problem to be solved.
They found a bed for her in the Palms.
She begged no, but what else could they do?

EVEN SO

Long ago, winds brought flights of butterflies;
chemicals and climate change make it
rare to see those lovely dancers now.
Yet I am happy that in the bright sky
squadrons of green parrots still make
a joyful racket – the raucous battle-cry of life

CLIMBING A COCONUT TREE

A poor thin boy sat with us at breakfast.
I thought nothing of it; our mother had brought him.
I greeted him but he was silent when I said hello.
My mother set before him a big bowl of porridge,
sweetened with helpings of muscovado.
He relished it with deliberate good manners, smiled,
told me he was going to climb for coconuts.
His father took them to Tunapuna market.
He told me how he climbed the tall and curving palms
with a leather strap. You had to have strong arms,
he said. The insteps of his feet sometimes bled raw.
I craved to learn and he said he would instruct me.
A hard skill in my mind; I called it an art.
I never saw him again. I never climbed for coconuts.

EBB AND FLOW OF THE UNIVERSE

The cruel pandemic begun in Wuhan
wreaked such havoc on our shores –
an important, memorable time.
I recall long ago a sharp rainstorm,
how the sun shone brilliantly afterwards
and water glistened in grass-pools
near the children's swing.
A beautiful hibiscus bush grew nearby,
I felt some yellowing, dying leaves disgraced it.
I pulled the sere and old off carefully,
leaving the lovely plant a perfect green,
except the marvel of its blood-red blossoms.

STRANGE MORNING ON THE RIVER

It began with song on the river-beach
from a young man in black who thought
he was alone. His song was pure as the wind
that rushed across the water. He stopped
when he saw me and I was sad.
I walked on as the sun rose in a vast blue sky,
passing a fishing boat beached not far away.
Men stood around in groups. I could not see
what they looked at. What's the catch? I asked.
No word, so I went myself to look.
Tangled in a fishing net, skull bones grinned at me.
They let the young boy through who had sung
his lonely song, now silent as a single leaf that falls.
He knelt and looked, wept bitter tears.
I asked but no one would tell the story.

LOW TIDE, HALF-MOON BAY

Rose-coloured curve of coast I loved,
the kindest harbour my boyhood ever knew,
of dawn-walks with sea-wind in my face,
watching gold-tipped waves move in, move in.
Congregating sandpipers on the shining beach
leave what looks like writing on the sand.
I thought what messages of hope
are lost when the rising sea returns.

WHAT ELSE?

I miss my friend, O'Meara.
Our talk-lit fire burned in our daily life.
What ever, what ever was tossed upon the flames
blazed anew – a fire that only life's routines put out.
When he was dying, we still talked long,
and then not so long as he grew weaker.
The last time, *What else, what else*, I cried.
No more. Old friend, this lifetime's not enough.

AMONG THE HUMMINGBIRDS

I sit among the hummingbirds
reading John Keats.
"All that summer he wrote poetry"
as if the whole of him was song,
as if the whole of him was starlight.
Never his like again.

TASTE OF WATER

I woke from the depths of sleep last night,
dust filling my throat with worry – a threat to life.
Sweet swallows from the glass kept near at hand
re-gifted life to me – a simple thing like that.
Out of the open window I saw a spray of stars,
brightening buds on the stem of night,
whose beauty and meaning I could not grasp.
A taste of water, how do I explain?

THE DAY STARTS WELL

I walked on that dawnlit Antiguan beach,
smelling tar from anchored fishing boats,
the sun just spreading its dance on the golden sea.
Idly, I picked up pretty shells, stones tumbled
into beauty by the waves, red-speckled
crab backs, twigs of whitened coral.
A young man passed, kicking up diamonds,
silvery fish on a string. "Good catch!" I shout.
He smiles with delight, dance steps in the surf.
Soon after, I found an old penny shone brightly by the sea.

RUG OF FIRE

In silver-buttoned satin-suit and Sunday best,
hair trimmed and shiningly in place,
I was the first-born ready to be presented
to the grandest great-aunt in all the family.
My mother and grandmother prepped
me to meet the grand old lady.
She was blind, would want to feel my face,
and I was told twice to kiss her cheek,
to whisper in her dark and cluttered rooms.
What I remember best was quite another thing:
the beauty of the framed carpets on the wall,
the rug I stepped on beneath her ancient chair,
bright orange cloths woven into flames,
and I recall her sweet smile and embrace,
not awkward at all, with fire at my feet.

THE PRINCE OF DARKNESS VISITS

When you come of age and start to learn
the social graces, are allowed among
and praised by friendly adults, I recall
one evening of a fierce storm – I never saw its like.
It thrashed wild among great garden trees,
put out all the lights of heaven.
The conversation could be of nothing else.
The thunder rolling ever nearer, then
a fiery crack, rain pouring down in blackest
sackfuls, an old aunt solemnly declared,
"The Prince of Darkness is about his work."
My thought-murmured, what a fart, what
almighty pissing! Dad caught my guilty eye
with a slight smile. I've wondered ever since.

HARDLY KNOWING WHAT I MEAN

Simply to go beyond the steppes of heaven,
venture far beyond the mountains of the sun,
where stars entangle endlessly, time beyond all time,
I find again the eternity of green forests I have loved,
a wandering shadow within white orchid caves,
the shining river waiting on a rising moon.
With shimmering necklaces of pearls my solitary delight,
how can I not remember the blessings of the earth,
those who love me and those whom I have loved?
The songs of Easter echo in my mind,
the voices of beloved children and their joyful laughter,
the old priest shouting Hallelujah in his last agony,
a one-legged beggar putting out a pustuled hand,
peacocks in a Persian garden parading before my eyes.
Hatred and the rage of life can never be subdued
except by the bravery of soldiers who will not guard the King.
Again, again, the laughter of children, the astonishments of love,
a radiance as of a fire burning beyond the curtain of the world…
I cannot go on. Beauty summons me to sadness.
Until all is forgotten, let me not forget.

RANDOM INVENTORY OF THE WORLD

Begin with slaughter in a score of countries.
A migrant father lifting his drowned son in his arms.
Waves lapping higher up the old kings' thrones.
A baby at her mother's breast at Mass this morning.
An old man carefully counting his change
at the bus stop by Conversation Tree.
There is more, but let us leave it there.
Well, add perhaps the melting of polar ice,
the red fury of trees on fire.

A TASTE OF TIME

When evening falls, I go out on the patio
with the crystal glass I drink good rum in –
15-year-Old El Dorado – with single cube of ice,
with hanging baskets of green fern around.
It's a perfect place to see the sun go down,
and indulge idle thoughts about how long
it takes a cube of ice to melt.
The world changes in less time than you think:
the sky a blaze of colours, red and gold,
then threads of silver and the trails of blue
darken into grey and then the night comes on.
Still the ice cube makes its hospitable sound
until a star appears, glittering in the blackness
a trillion miles away, and ice has melted into rum,
and sharp, the good taste of life delights me.

MY WIFE BUYS A SILK DRESS

I rarely shop with my wife –
it's boring waiting around so much.
She's trying on shoes, dresses, choosing, choosing,
but not deciding and never done with it.
Good Lord! An hour past and nothing bought.
So, I go to the coffee shop
and read well-written *Economist* obituaries.
One time, though, she shopped with me.
I wanted nuts and bolts and a leather belt;
she found a rack and bought a silk dress,
pleased with its perfect fit. A lucky day.
On the way out of a bookstall, tucked away,
unbelievably, was Gerard Manley Hopkins' Letters.

A SENSE OF LONGING

Life is so short. I write this in my 90th year
and say it for a reason. All of today
has been a rare occurrence, the sun
slanting through the window,
glistening on the African violets.
I've been sent brilliant, vivid pictures
of butterflies caught on the hills of Mount St. Benedict,
hunted amidst the poui trees of my boyhood.
My wife has made me an omelette – cheese
and chopped mushrooms – I've never tasted before.
Even routines can be new. I looked in the mirror,
combed my hair differently, heard the grandchildren
clattering up the stairs. *Look, look what we found!*
What is it? Whatever it is, it is happiness,
and the day not even a quarter over.

LILIES OF THE FIELD

God-emperors heedless come and go,
the raw brutalities of life proceed.
On all sides barricades are manned.
Victory or death! men wave and shout.
Defiant women whisper other things.
A bright boy, eyes smiling in the news,
drowned canoeing on Algonquin Lake.
Comets stream across the universe.
My son who gardens in the city parks,
reports today they planted lilies.
An old lady stopped and praised the work.

SOMETIMES I HEAR THE RAINFALL SINGING

Sometimes I heard the rainfall singing,
but it was not the rain, it was my mother's voice
in the room next to mine, at her needlework
or fixing the baby's clothes, making up her cot,
everything done with love — everything my mother did
she did with love. She sang with such a sense of happiness —
which is why I find the rain's voice comforting.
All my boyhood: it was my mother singing.

GOLDEN ORANGES OF ESPERANZA

He showed me with pride the mounds
of golden oranges for collection at Esperanza,
the best of all our fruit, he said,
planted with care, manured to perfection,
well-tended in uncrowded rows.
There's nothing better than the earth made fruitful.
I saw my father's joy at the Union Club
when crops were good. No doubt it was the money,
but how he told me suggested something more.

THE RED LOCUST

A red-winged locust lands upon my arm
dropped out of green leaves above.
It shows a blood-mark on my skin,
it spreads its rose-red wings to go,
a poem I can never write.

OF COURSE

A friend is coming soon
to show us his red macaw.
Mary has sliced green mangoes,
so good with salt and pepper.
In the shadow of a rainbow
the children are dancing.

NO TEARS ARE LEFT

Sad bells tolled across the river,
clouds like sorrow piling pale and grey;
the young man who gardened at the monastery
died so young we could not believe it.
When he was gone, his green beds withered,
the red fruit dropped, wasted on the ground.
The honeybees still sizzle in the sun-filled air,
but who will tend them in their golden hives?
The sweetest natured man I ever knew,
his mother placed her hands across his face
before they closed his casket.
"How I will miss you, my dear son,
how I will miss your greeting in the morning,
how I will miss the laughter of little children
rushing to greet you in the wind-fresh afternoon,
how I will miss you, my son who cared for me,
you were so good to me, my son."
Down the great river the grey clouds weep.

ALONE

The moon rises in full splendour,
glowing abyss through a needle slit.
The old trees shake gleaming in the wind;
leaves drift down caught in light.
In the distance, over the pale sea wall,
wave-caps dance in the vast night.
Far-far out the silence has no end;
around me, moonlight in an empty room.

MORTON

Morton was just under four feet tall, hunched back,
brown face tucked down in his shoulders,
but his eyes always smiling as if the world
was sparkling in his sight. He got about all right,
nimble in fact, worked for Guyana Power and Light,
got up the tall poles, adept as anyone.
I think Morton was never sorry for himself.
He aged quickly, though, and soon GP&L retired him.
I gave him odd jobs around our house.
He kept our cars gleaming clean, care in all he did,
determined to be perfect. He liked to talk cricket
and the GPL – he'd helped fix transformers
after they exploded, showed me a yellowing picture
of him as a little hero. But his genes destroyed him.
He was done at fifty, ended at the Palms.
I helped him get a wheelchair which he
manoeuvred adroitly. To the end he talked cheerfully –
but often thoughts would come to me unbidden.
Who will ever know how often in his life
he was tall and straight and able
to put out his hand to me in a level line?

STRANGE BEAUTY

Strange birdsong woke me one morning,
a loveliness I never heard before,
repeated many times, then it departed.
I have never heard that song again.
Time passes but I do not want it named.
There is beauty in not knowing what one loves

HIBISCUS

Cold in the night wind, alone under the crowded stars,
I counted one hundred hibiscus in the garden,
every one beautiful. One day's light they last,
adorn the world and are gone. Ninety years
the same — at least it seems so at the end.

NIGHT WATCHMAN

There was a time when I looked for encounters,
wanting to know what others did, that I didn't.
I'd stop by a shop, talk with the night guard there,
asked what he loved in life when he was not at work.
Well, he said, *I love songbirds from the forest,
have them at home and love to train them.*
How do you train wild birds? Of course, I asked.
I know whistles. I teach them, I am a master.
Whistle one for me, I asked. In truth, he whistled well.
Then a truck came up with a delivery and he had to stop.
Later, I tried to find him again, but he'd moved on.

FALLING DOWN THE STAIRS IN MY 90TH YEAR

I slipped on the mopped stairs,
cracked two ribs, not much, surely,
but gravity is a heavy weapon.
The value of breathing becomes known –
coughing measured in decibels of pain
with poisonous spiders walking in my chest.
Horizontal sleep becomes dangerous territory
and getting vertical a steep and challenging climb,
inching from here to uneven there.
Towelling the backbone dry, lifting a basket of fruit:
who would have thought so many simple actions
have to be assisted? Make the best of it,
give thanks warmly, nice helpless old man.
But beware that role too soon!

THE ANNIHILATED WORLD

I woke suddenly in a dream
in a place of savage thorn-trees.
The window framed half a moon,
only half a moon, and a blood-red
whisper in my mind said
everything was chopped in half.
I was aching, the bed strangely hard.
It was not the muscle of the heart
but some new 90-year affliction.
I went to the window slowly,
stood silently with that mysterious pain,
a feeling of tremendous loss,
with so little time left in the world.
"Dry your eyes," I thought:
a great storm had been reported,
a strong wind from the seawall.
I stood among desperate people
on a stricken shore.

IT ALL BEGINS AGAIN

The birds this morning
summon me to life again.
I have felt dull these past days,
very old, with the endless loneliness
of death in sight,
and the marvellous shadows of the sky
said nothing to me.
But now, the air is sweet with song;
outside, the sun shines golden
through green branches moving in the wind –
honeycombs of light, joy indeed,
the whole garden I so love
an altar cloth of flowers.

ABOUT THE AUTHOR

Ian McDonald was born in Trinidad April 18th 1933. He was educated at Queens Royal College, Guyana and Clare College, Cambridge University (1951-55). In 1955 he joined Bookers in the then British Guiana, and spent 52 years in the sugar industry, becoming Director of Marketing & Administration with Bookers and continuing with GuySuCo after nationalization in 1976, until 1999. Between 2000 – 2007 he was CEO of the Sugar Association of the Caribbean. He was an Editorial Consultant with the West Indian Commission, 1991-92. In January 2009 he was appointed Chairman of Guyana Publications Inc., publishers of *Stabroek News*.

As a lawn tennis player he played at Wimbledon, captained Cambridge, Guyana and the West Indian Davis Cup team in the 1960s. He was Guyana's Sportsman of the Year in 1957.

He has published seven poetry collections (*Mercy Ward*, *Essequibo*, *Jaffo the Calypsonian*, *Between Silence and Silence*, *Selected Poem*, *The Comfort of All Things*, *River Dancer* and *Collected Poems*), and prose collections of essays and speeches, *A Cloud of Witnesses* and *A Love of Poetry*. His novel *The Humming-Bird Tree* was published in 1969 and was made into a BBC film in 1992. He won the Guyana Prize for Literature – for poetry – in 1992, 2004, and 2012. He edited the magazine *Kyk-Over-Al* from 1984 to 2000. He edited: *AJS at 70: The Collected Poems of A.J. Seymour* with Jacqueline de Weever and *The Heinemann Book of Caribbean Poetry in English,* with Stewart Brown; with Lloyd Searwar, Joel Benjamin and Laxshmi Kallicharan he contributed to compiling *They Came in Ships*, an anthology of Indo-Guyanese writing and he edited *The Bowling Was Superfine*, an anthology of West Indian cricket writing, with Stewart Brown. In 2008 his *Selected Poems* was shortlisted for the Royal Society of Literature Ondaatje Literary Prize. His one-act play, *The Tramping Man*, produced in Guyana in 1969, was published by UWI's School of Continuing Studies in *A Time and a Season: 8 Caribbean Plays*. His weekly column, "Ian on Sunday" has appeared in *Stabroek News* for thirty years.

He has written extensively on cricket and in 2005 delivered the

Inaugural Lecture entitled "Cricket: A Hunger in the West Indian Soul" in the Sir Frank Worrell lecture series. He was a member of a panel set up by the West Indies Cricket Board in 2007 to report and make recommendations on the governance of West Indies Cricket. He assisted in the compilation and production of *Cricket At Bourda*, celebrating the Georgetown Cricket Club, in time for the World Cup, March 2007.

He was elected a Fellow of the Royal Society of Literature in 1970, received the Golden Arrow of Achievement Guyana national award (1986) and in 1997 the University of the West Indies conferred on him an Honorary Doctorate of Letters for services to sugar, sport and literature. He contributed, with his sister Robin McDonald, to the publication of their mother's memoir, *Beloved, Memoir by Thelma Seheult*, published by Paria Publishing in Trinidad, 2016, and also to their father's memoir, *Archie, the Memoir. An Abounding Joy*, a collection of essays on cricket and sport, edited by Professor Clem Seecharan was published by Hansib in 2018. He and his wife, Mary Angela, have two sons, Jamie and Darren, and he has a son Keith from a previous marriage.

ALSO BY IAN McDONALD

New and Collected Poems
ISBN: 9781845234034; pp. 448; pub. 2018; price £17.99

From the earliest poems published in the 1950s, Ian McDonald has been a distinctive and admired voice in Caribbean poetry. This volume brings together all his published collections: *Jaffo the Calypsonian*, *Mercy Ward*, *Essequibo*, *Between Silence and Silence*, *The Comfort of All Things* and *River Dancer*. In addition, there are almost two books' worth of new poems, the product of a remarkable flowering of inspiration and memory that visited Ian McDonald in his eighties.

The poems reflect both a changing Caribbean world and changes in the witnessing self, though there are consistencies of vision. Few Caribbean poets have so sensuously observed the region's natural world, but have also been aware of the dangers of the "gilding eye" glossing over the poverty which is still the lot of so many Caribbean people. Poems celebrate the pleasures of good company, love, marriage, children, food, gardens and books, but set against this the knowledge that whilst his has been a life that has contributed much to the good of the region, it has also been one of the privilege of material security and whiteness. Many poems display a compassionate concern with the suffering of Guyana's poor, particularly in the stark realism of the *Mercy Ward* poems.

There is also an inward eye, aware of the passing years. From the son who sees his parents' ageing, the father of growing children, the keen sportsman facing the decline of middle age, and the man facing his own later years of health anxieties, though nourished by a loving wife, attentive grandchildren and the pleasures of the garden. All these phases of life return to the poetry of the past few years.

ABOUT US

Peepal Tree Press has been decolonising bookshelves since 1985 with our focus on Caribbean and Black British writing. We are a wholly independent publisher and part of the Arts Council of England's national portfolio since 2015. In 2024, we established a partnership with HopeRoad Publishing.

Peepal Tree's list features fiction, poetry and non-fiction, including academic texts and creative memoirs. By the end of 2024, we will have published 490 books by 320 different authors, including those published in our anthologies. Most of our titles remain in print. Our books have won the Costa Prize, T.S. Eliot, Forward, OCM Bocas, Guyana and Casa de las Americas prizes.

From the beginning, women and LGBTI authors have been fully represented in our lists. We have focused on the new by publishing many first-time authors and have restored to print important Caribbean books in all genres in our Caribbean Classics Series. We have also published overlooked material from the past as a way of challenging received ideas about the Caribbean canon.

We see decolonisation as about overthrowing and repairing oppressive, economically exploitative and racist power relationships. Many of our books explore the halting, difficult process of overcoming four hundred years of colonialism in the Caribbean in the post-independence period. But we also see decolonisation as needing to happen in Britain. We are committed to ending British amnesia over the destructiveness of empire and colonialism, including our role in the irreparable damage of nearly three centuries of slavery , and promoting an understanding of how Britain's long relationship with the Caribbean has contributed to the making of British society in ways that persist into the present. As a publisher, we have taken a stand on supporting Palestinian rights for freedom from a colonial occupation and denial of statehood. We hope that you enjoyed reading this book as much as we did publishing it. Your purchase supports writers to flourish. Keep in touch with our newsletter at https://www.peepaltreepress.com/subscribe, and discover all our books at www.peepaltreepress.com, and join us on social media @peepaltreepress